"…Many full-colo
likely to appeal b
behavior and char

"You and the peop
to the geese raisin
people, young and
mammals, insects
the connection. I

"I love the story. T
Canada geese. By
supporting biosph

—Dr. Lo
Warrio

"Kudos to Barbar

"We are enjoying

—JoJo

"A lovely book an
well into the story
original nesting g
animals."

SECRET LIVES OF
WILD CANADA GEESE

A true love story in their hidden paradise

BARBARA KLIDE

Bijou
Publishing

Folsom, California

Bijou Publishing
705 E Bidwell St., Ste. 2-418
Folsom, CA 95630
www.BijouPublishing.com

ISBN 978-1-7365475-2-6 soft cover
ISBN 978-1-7365475-4-0 hard cover
ISBN 978-1-7365475-3-3 ebook

Book Design - Andy Grachuk - www.JingotheCat.com
Cover Design – Anita Jones - www.AnotherJones.com
Cover photography – Barbara Klide

All photographs, except where noted, were taken by Barbara Klide.

Although the author has made every effort to ensure that the information in this book is accurate, some "accounts of events" and photographs, distinct from the author's own, were freely and graciously provided with express oral or implied consent for publication and the author is not responsible for any misrepresentation.

An earlier edition of this material was published in two separate volumes in 2018.

Publisher's Cataloging-In-Publication Data
(Prepared by The Donohue Group, Inc.)

Names: Klide, Barbara, author, photographer.
Title: Secret lives of wild Canada geese : a true love story in their hidden paradise / Barbara Klide.
Description: Folsom, California : Bijou Publishing, [2022] | Includes bibliographical references.
Identifiers: ISBN 9781736547526 (softcover) | ISBN 9781736547540 (hardcover) | ISBN 9781736547533 (ebook)
Subjects: LCSH: Canada goose--California--Pictorial works. | Animals and civilization--California--Pictorial works. | Urban animals--California--Pictorial works. | LCGFT: Illustrated works.
Classification: LCC QL696.A52 K55 2022 (print) | LCC QL696.A52 (ebook) | DDC 598.41--dc23

Printed in the United States of America

Dedication

T he events inspiring this story about a little family of geese touched many people and brought to light a side of them that is not often seen in a business environment.

To all the wonderful people who witnessed the unfolding story and engaged in constant chatter, opening their compassionate hearts and sharing their thoughts with childlike glee, and especially to those people who cherished the geese and stepped forward to make our friends' lives safe and their stay comfortable.

Acknowledgements

We are immensely grateful for the acceptance of the Canada geese by all the people working around this campus including both the CEO, Tim Burke, at Quest Technology Management, and Ann Nguyen, CEO, at Cokeva, Inc. These adjoining businesses in Roseville, California share the courtyard where the geese made themselves at home.

Special thanks to my two copy editors, Amy Comi and Molly Burke. I am grateful for their ability to perform a sanity check, and as stern grammarians, tidying up past perfect, simple past, and continuous tenses, after my occasional carefree jaunt around the English language.

Special thanks to Steve Hill and Bryce Hill, father and son who rescued the two eyas described in the story.

A portion of the profits will be donated to several organizations all which are dedicated to the animals that share our world. They include Sacramento Audubon Society, California Raptor Center, FieldHaven Feline Center, Fat Kitty City Humane Society, Lockwood Animal Rescue Center–Wolves and Combat Veterans (LARC) as seen on Animal Planet, Let 'em Run Foundation for Wild Mustangs (LERF).

Table of Contents

Prologue

*"Unadulterated, unsweetened observations are what the
real nature-lover craves."*

John Burroughs, American naturalist and nature essayist

Year One: Along Came Ryan, the Little Gosling King

This is the true saga of an indescribably magnificent pair of mated
Canada geese whose migration flyway north took them to their own
secret paradise—a business courtyard. The pair lived as they wished,
raising a family in this lush and unusual site for many months, though
we questioned its suitability. The geese, however, were resolute and
not only made it work, but thrived.

In this charming slice of life, our wild animal friends unexpectedly
intersected with humans and a palpable, warm fondness for them
washed over us all. We pressed our noses against glass, close up and
personal, and witnessed their lives with amazement.

The committed pair proved to be nature's Zen masters, enjoying the
present moment and brushing off trouble when it visited—and visit
it did. In the end, the geese taught us important lessons including
harmony, tolerance, friendship, family, survival, and the simple joys
of life.

We were thrilled and honored to welcome our incomparable guests,
the noble, sensitive, caring, and lovable Canada geese.

Year Two: The Return of the Geese

Wild geese are driven by instinctive seasonal routines like all of the animal kingdom. In fact, we learned in the first year, that Canada geese are highly philopatric meaning that they are wired to return to their former nesting ground. Knowing that, we excitedly hoped and waited for, then joyously celebrated, their homecoming the following year. That was the expectation that we had for our friends—but were they really the same mated pair?

What we did know was that the return of the geese was no less captivating. Everything was new again yet wildly different. We watched, addicted to the family dramas, intrigue, and cliffhangers—much like a good soap opera, only these storylines were real.

Barbara Klide

Aerial view of courtyard © 2018 Google

"To sit in the shade on a fine day and look upon verdure is the most perfect refreshment." - Jane Austen, Mansfield Park

Part 1
Year One
Along Came Ryan, the Little Gosling King

Introduction and a Cooper's Hawk

"I began to reflect on Nature's eagerness to sow life everywhere, to fill the planet with it, to crowd with it the earth, the air, and the seas. Into every corner, into all forgotten things and nooks."

Henry Beston, American writer and naturalist

April 20

We had heard her shrieks before, *kee-eeeee-arr, kee-eeeee-orr!* This time she was *not* announcing her presence. Tearing through the leafy canopies, the hawk's silence was menacing. One of fourteen raptor species in the Sacramento, California region, the Cooper's Hawk's red eyes focused like lasers on a tiny, golden goose; a gosling not yet fledged—with no feathers for flight. Even if it could fly, there would be no contest as the powerfully agile predator can reach a flight speed of 55 miles per hour.

Behind office window glass, people watched in fear as the hawk emerged from the trees racing for the open with her wings spread full and her legs out. She dipped low for a split second, and then startlingly swept away from the gosling, rocketing high and gliding over the building out of sight.

On the lawn below, the baby's parents fiercely defended their offspring, honking with necks outstretched, and slapping their wings. On full guard, they tolerated no nonsense today. Everyone breathed a sigh of relief. The little goose family was safe once again. We knew that the hawk would soon return to the enclosed courtyard, often called the "quad," as her own nest of hungry chicks was located just outside of it.

Only one gosling hatched after many eggs were laid. We called him Ryan like the actor, Ryan Gosling (after the Canadian actor). It seemed momentarily funny, but it stuck. We endearingly named Ryan's Mom "Mother Goose," the imaginary author of children's nursery rhymes, often depicted as a goose. We named the male gander "Hawkeye"—like the lead actor in the TV series "Mash," or the Marvel Comics superhero, or the protagonist in the book, "Last of the Mohicans," take your pick.

Within 24 hours of hatching, goose parents lead their goslings to open water where they are able to dive and swim 30-40 feet underwater. Unable to fly out of the quad until he is two or three months old and fully fledged, little Ryan could not enjoy any lakes or rivers, as he was plainly "landlocked." Still, life seemed sweet for the three of them with an automatic sprinkler system providing water and an abundance of grass for the geese, primarily vegetarians, to eat continuously.

The people working in the buildings frequently stared out into the courtyard hoping to catch a glimpse of the wonderful little baby, so full of life and impossibly cute. They fretted for the family's safety as the geese were "sitting ducks," so exposed and vulnerable, knowing that in one moment the possibility of death loomed large. Will the geese survive, let alone thrive?

Quad-courtyard

The lawn-covered quad is encased within a pair of connecting buildings housing two separate businesses. One is a data center containing all the essential servers, power sources, and people to support data. That is where I work. The other business is also a technology firm.

Quest Technology Management

The entire structure, including the quad, sits on a large, quiet plot of industrial acreage with other buildings and sports fields used throughout the year. With so many animals making their homes there, including over three dozen small bird species, many people refer to it as the "wild kingdom." There are hummingbirds galore attracted to the bottlebrush bushes with their colorful flowers, shrubs and trees planted to adorn the data center's façade. Occasionally, doves land on the ledge of a window cooing and peering inside as if to offer a friendly greeting of peace.

Jack rabbits frequently skitter about or nap on the lawn in front of our building—under the very tree housing the hawk's nest. The baby jack rabbits called "kits," like the turkey chicks and other birds, are easy prey for big raptors like hawks, but their larger parents seem relatively safe. We also see lizards, butterflies, and wasps—whose nests must be cleared from the building eaves occasionally. Feral cats periodically roam around and while coyotes live in the region, none have been reported on the grounds. Last, but not least, geese in flight (called a "skein") or geese in V formation (called a "wedge"), fly over the data center, north in spring and south in fall, signaling the changing seasons.

The rectangular quad itself, short for quadrangle, is 250 by 160 feet, slightly smaller than an average 45 thousand square foot soccer field. From the sky, it may have seemed like a safe place for a mated pair of geese to nest with its many shade trees around the perimeter, its vast lawn, and reliable source of water, but it was far from ideal. **Here is where our story actually begins...**

30 days earlier... March 20, Spring

For reasons known only to them, Mother Goose and Hawkeye decided to nest on the roof of a small structure, not unlike a bus stop. Located inside the quad along a glass wall, they shelter people sitting outside on their breaks or lunch. With no time to spare, nest building atop the structure began.

Few people knew that the geese had "landed", or of their nest hidden above view, but word of it quickly spread. It was anybody's guess what

Roof nesting site - inside Quad

material was used to make the nest. In the wild, a goose uses mosses, lichens, twigs, and leaves, or the nest is built from a large mound of grass and cattail stems. The goose creates a soft lining with fuzzy feathers, called down, which she pulls out from her chest. Whatever material Mother Goose used, we all wondered about the anticipated set of eggs, a "clutch," that she would lay, and we waited impatiently knowing that it takes some 30 days of incubation before they would hatch.

No one saw what happened next, but many people suspected that the hawk, or maybe an owl, tried to steal the eggs, as we would often find broken eggs on the ground. The typical number of eggs geese lay is five or six, but she could have laid up to a dozen. Perhaps the predators dropped the snatched eggs after a bitter fight. We believed that the geese were determined to battle to the last egg, and that's just what they did.

Just shy of 30 days later, and with great fanfare, along came Ryan! He was the only gosling to hatch. What a day that was! Goslings can walk within hours of hatching and the baby may have flown or fallen off the roof trying to follow his parents. With their fluff and small size they can fall or "flutter" down about two stories without injury; any higher and the goslings would have to be rescued. There are many online videos* showing wildlife rescuers, or just good Samaritans, gathering goslings in cat or dog carriers with the goose parents following them even into an elevator going down, through a lobby, and out to a park where they are released and appear practically giddy for their deliverance!

*SEE RESOURCES SECTION

We don't know exactly how he got down, but baby Ryan's appearance surprised and thrilled everyone. Talk about him and his parents exploded as if it were a birth in our own family. He was after all, a perfect,

little, golden baby. People started taking pictures left and right because he was, well, adorable and his photogenic parents were wildly majestic and graceful with their distinguished black heads, bill, and long necks with a striking white patch or "chinstrap."

From then on, Mom and Dad paraded the gosling around their private paradise, showing off little Ryan while teaching and rearing him in this secluded area.

I call this shot Abbey Road

Under normal circumstances, the goose and gander move the goslings to a "brood rearing area." Both parents take an active role in their care and protection. Often, several family groups rear brood flocks in the same vicinity called "crèches," where the parents teach the young geese to fly in the water and on land. Constant practice with their wings outstretched strengthens their young bodies and helps them gain confidence.

How in the world Ryan would learn to fly in this unusual schoolyard was a mystery and became a growing concern.

Most days, Ryan delighted in the sunshine and the adoration of his Mom and Dad and sometimes stayed warm under Mom's wings in rainy or chilly weather. From behind panes of glass, the people admired the devoted parents and were completely captivated by the baby mascot. When outside, we kept our distance to avoid Ryan inadvertently imprinting on us*. Known to follow anything that moves, including dogs, ducks, and people, goslings are highly impressionable. There is a beautiful movie called "Fly Away Home" that showcases a true story about Canada geese imprinting on humans.

*SEE RESOURCES SECTION

While people enjoyed watching the geese, they also started buzzing with ideas about how to help them. A few called wildlife rescue groups, but found that unless an animal was injured, or stuck on a tall building, rescue staff could not be spared as they were overwhelmed with more serious local animal issues. Some workers at the site thought the situation for our goose family *was* desperate, but others felt sure nature would run its course in time. Concerned, but hopeful, some secretly imagined the geese staying for good, but unless migratory geese are injured, they never become resident geese.

Photo by Bryce Hill

So, mesmerized by the goose family, people frequently forgot to swipe their identification badges on the corridor doors paralleling the glass windows along the quad. That meant that a security alarm would go off—every time! Setting off the alarm, "set off" the security staff too, who rolled their eyes when called to reset the door alarm. The geese were such a novelty at the beginning that we suffered blaring alarms two or three times a day!

Learning about Geese

"Ask the beasts and they will teach you the beauty of this earth."

St. Francis of Assisi, Founder of the Franciscan Order Patron of Animals and Animal Lovers

Some people read up on geese and shared that they are monogamous, loyal, and emotional, with the adults finding a mate for life and staying with their babies until they can fly. Further, if a family member or a mate is injured, geese will stay with and guard them until they recover or die.

The average age of Canada geese is 10-25 years in the wild. Some live to 30 and in captivity can reach up to 40 years. They are the largest geese in the world weighing up to 25 pounds, are about 45 inches in length, and have a wingspan of nearly 75 inches. During migration season, which is October through March, geese typically fly 40 miles per hour and can reach up to 70 miles per hour if they catch a strong tailwind. Their flight range can be two to three thousand miles, and they know their habitats well.

Where we live, the Sacramento Valley, rice fields provide wildlife habitat to geese and over 200 other species. These ricelands create wetlands with an abundance of food. Geese are also seen nesting around golf courses and park ponds and have adapted well to civilization. There is a wealth of information you can learn on the California Rice Commission (CalRice) and the National Audubon Society websites, which you can find in the Resources Section.

To remain healthy, especially for flight, geese preen, keeping their feathers clean and dry at all times. They do this by pulling their feathers one by one, removing dirt and allowing air to flow through them. They also use their bills and head to rub oil over their feathers, which they get from an oil gland near the base of their tail. This oiling process helps keep the birds free of parasites, insulated, and dry. Our little Ryan dutifully began working on his feathers following the example of his parents.

We also learned that geese have been around since about ten million years ago in the Miocene geological epoch when the apes arose, human ancestors split from chimpanzees, and bears, deer, whales, seals, and kelp spread around the globe.

Finally, the Canada geese are federally protected by the Migratory Bird Treaty Act of 1918 between the U.S. and Great Britain (for Canada) with later amendments to include Mexico, Japan, and the "Soviet Union" (now the Russian Federation). The act also established hunting seasons. Collectively we learned so much about these magnificent creatures thanks to Ryan and his parents choosing to call our quad home for a season.

Name Change?

"What's in a name? That which we call a rose by any other name would smell as sweet."

William Shakespeare, English playwright, poet, and actor

One person who observed the geese regularly called Ryan "Pancake," which was awfully cute. Seems that the butter-yellow gosling was lying in the warm sun one day with his legs spread behind him, bone structure flat, very much like a pancake. Well, I suppose one could call the baby "Pancake" if one wishes.

Then there was the other issue…maybe Ryan was a female! So we figured, as an alternative, we would call the gosling, Rihanna, like the singer—might as well have a celebrity female name to match the male actor's name. Ryan has of late become a popular name for girls as well as boys, so we decided to keep the name regardless. It should be pointed out that "Ryan" happens to be a classic Irish last name meaning "little king." That sealed the deal!

Turkeys

―――○―――

"Kinship with all creatures of the earth, sky, and water was a real and active principle."

Chief Luther Standing Bear, Sicangu and Oglala Lakota chief, Native American author, educator, philosopher, and actor

We have occasionally seen a group of turkey hens fly into the courtyard, amble about, and then fly away. Sometimes, one of the birds would get left behind. We speculated about the dubious intelligence of any lone turkey after seeing it stare at its reflection in the glass windows, perhaps thinking she was not truly alone. She would stay for hours admiring the "fairest one of all" in the looking glass. Once, however, one of those dilly-dallying turkeys got too close to Ryan and there was a brief, but nasty little scuffle. The geese made it clear that the turkey crossed a line and she eventually flew away. We saw less of the hens as the territorial geese acted like they owned the place. According to the people, they did.

―――○―――

April 26

Not to be outdone by the hens visiting the quad, the tom turkeys appeared at the front entrance to the data center and frequently photobombed architectural photo shoots of the facility. They loved strutting their stuff even more so than the geese. They are most interesting neighbors and had made their home here long before any of us!

War

"The supreme art of war is to subdue the enemy without fighting."

Sun Tzu, c. 5th century. BC, Chinese general and military strategist

May 11

One day I saw a pair of geese on the entrance roof and my heart sank. That could only mean that the baby was taken by a predator and the parents had deserted the quad. Several of us made a beeline to the quad windows. We needed to know for sure. We saw no geese at the southwest end, but you can't see the entire area unless you pass through all the security doors down the length of the glassed corridor—a long haul. It felt like forever as we ran, looking outside every step of the way. We were "badging" through the doors as fast as we could. Finally, as we passed the last door at the northwest end, we all looked outside. To our immense delight, resting on a door mat, safe and oblivious to our breathless fears, was the little family. I nearly cried for joy.

Not all was calm, however. No sooner were we filled with relief, when the geese jumped up in alarm. The parents charged toward the middle of the quad and the little one was running with his short legs as fast as he could. Now what? What could have disturbed the peace? So, we ran back again following the action. We tore through the locked doors badging back in one-by-one looking outside the windows for the answer. Very quickly, we found it. Those two geese we saw on the roof, who we mistook for the parents, were invaders! They had flown off the roof and landed in the quad causing a major commotion for our little family. Geese are only territorial during the short nesting season and what we saw was a textbook display in action—war!

The adults began posturing, which is a precursor to battle. They were tearing towards each other and a vicious fight for dominance ensued amid hisses, snarls, growls, and deafening honks while they slapped each other with their strong wings. In the confusion of battle, the parents even charged one another by accident until they realized they were are on the same team. We couldn't help wonder if a moment like this generated the expression "silly goose." Though, when you learn that bicyclists mimic the flying formation of geese by lining up in a race to overcome wind resistance, you gain newfound respect for geese savvy. These smart geese also have a remarkable "secret" for staying aloft—be sure to read about this phenomenon, called "lift."* But I digress…

*SEE RESOURCES SECTION

Through the mêlée, Ryan Gosling ran back and forth flapping his little wings a mile a minute, copying his parents' moves. It occurred to us this might have been war lesson 101 for the gosling. Either way, Mother Goose was battling for sure. She was on equal turf with her mate, Hawkeye. The fight went on for a good, long time until Mother Goose and Hawkeye successfully chased the invaders down to the south end of the quad where they clashed even more. After persistent charging, the parents prevailed and at last, the invaders were chased into flight over the building in a dramatic, crushing retreat. Everything settled down rather quickly for the family. They shook off the intrusion with evident ease and began to snack on grass. Just another day in the life… meanwhile, the people inside worried desperately for the family. Could they handle any more of these upsets? What was to come of them and especially Ryan Gosling?

From the right, the invaders plan their attack

Marching off to war

Posturing—a precursor to battle

Getting too close to the geese has its challenges – when a goose feels threatened, it will stretch out its neck, honk loudly, and may attack.

See short video of Ryan and parents in Resources Section - "Along Came Ryan"

21

Growing Strong... and Alone

"The most terrible poverty is loneliness, and the feeling of being unloved."

Mother Mary Teresa Bojaxhiu, Saint Teresa of Calcutta,
Albanian-Indian nun and missionary

May 15

By May the gosling was transforming even faster. Over one weekend, when most of us were home, Ryan, the Little King, went from a soft downy baby to a teenager with the first appearance of tiny flight feathers right on schedule at about eight weeks. We considered escorting the little family through the courtyard door to the other side, but there was no safe area or body of water for the parents to finish raising the gosling. More importantly, he still could not fly.

The geese also transformed the courtyard with their constant eating; we were keenly aware of the increasing mess that they let behind. Their daily rounds covered the courtyard, leaving debris in their wake in nearly equal amounts to what they ate—an adult goose can eat up to four pounds of grass per day! With two adults and a growing teen, the concrete walkways needed a strong power wash. Since all they eat is grass, the rain would wash away any mess except near the windows, a space protected by a roof overhang designed to throw rain water clear of the walls. The rainy season, now over, only lasts from the end of September to the end of May. The grassy area, though, was self-maintained thanks to the sprinkler system and the hot sun.

We were just starting to feel less anxious about the little fellow as he was getting big. Then one day, we realized with grave concern that the parents were gone! Where did they go and why? We read that the parents occasionally go off to feed, but will always return. To our utter happiness, by the end of the work day, they did. For a while, however, the parents would take off, one at a time, and sometimes the two would leave for many hours together. It became the norm, but we felt uneasy about this turn of events. We presumed that the parents taught Ryan enough to survive in his current environment, so that they could leave him alone, but their time away stretched longer and longer.

As we continued to dig for more answers, we learned that molting season was soon to start. The parents would lose all their flying feathers in about 30-45 days, right after nesting season when they are done brooding, rearing, and migrating. This annual process allows geese to grow new feathers to replace those that were lost, frayed, or worn after a year.

Before we realized that the parents would leave, the good people on the other side of the quad brought out some food. Eating the grasses and the leaves they "pruned" from all the bushes around the center court just didn't seem to be enough, or so we thought. The Little King took to the new treat, quickly enjoying a bucket filled with cracked corn and some hen scratch which contained added wheat, barley, and oats. Contrary to popular belief, providing grain to geese does not interrupt their ability to forage nor does it distort their migration abilities or schedule. Geese seem to have their "act together" no matter what.

May 23

Alone again, Little Ryan was often seen in repose alongside a wall, contentedly eating, walking around, or resting in the shade. We worried that he was quite lonely as geese are extremely social creatures and prayed that his parents would return soon to check on him.

May 25

With his parents gone, Ryan appeared to be completely abandoned even though we read that geese parents will NEVER do that. We thought they were waiting for him to fully fledge and be able to fly away with them, but the truth was the parents started molting as expected. Instinctively, they knew when they had fully molted, they wouldn't be able to fly, so they had to leave and if they didn't, they would be stuck. Oh, what a dilemma!

I was going to be on vacation for two weeks, so I wouldn't be able to monitor Ryan's activities except through the news I would hear from others when I checked in with email or phone calls. I had an aching feeling knowing that I would miss the handsome fellow.

I am a handsome fellow, aren't I?

Turkeys... Again!

"Of all possessions a friend is the most precious."
Herodotus, 5th century B.C. Greek historian and author

June 12

While I was gone, I received reports that the Little King was still very much alone, and that is how I found him when I returned. Every day, he would move around from one spot to the next, alone, just lying down or eating. Then one day, one person said that Ryan was extremely agitated. It was frightening. He was running back and forth along a perimeter. What was going on? It was highly troubling because he was usually so calm.

A person badged outside to the quad to watch and listen and then heard it...clucking! A lot of clucking! There were turkey hens on the other side of the building completely out of sight and they were loud. You could almost hear them say, "Hey there, we're out here and we know you're in there!" And that little boy understood—we know he did—and he wanted desperately to join in whatever the turkeys were doing to rescue himself from his abject loneliness.

The hens were probably just curious, causing mischief while they were simply hanging out and feeding. Those turkeys!

Baby's Own Spa!

"...In the glow of the glorious weather, In the sweet-scented, sensuous air, my burdens seem light as a feather – They are nothing to bear..."

Ella Wheeler Wilcox, American author and poet

When the geese first appeared on the scene, a sprinkler system was set up separate from the one buried under the dirt that kept the lawn watered. This new sprinkler became "the office water cooler." The little family would head to it daily. It was absolutely hysterical watching Ryan run to and fro through the sprinklers flapping his wings. He would do so with such abandon that all our hearts leapt for joy just watching him. Eventually, our neighbors delivered a kiddie pool to add to the geese's pleasure, especially since the days were getting hotter. It took a long time for him to figure out how to get into the pool, as at that time, he was just a short, little gosling. When his parents left and he grew large enough to easily hop in, he must have poked a hole in the pool with his bill because it began to leak. Unusable, it had to be replaced with a sturdier model. His first time in the new pool was another riot. He swam and dunked under the water with his feet and tail feathers high up in the air. While he couldn't fly and had nobody to teach him, like fish to water, this gosling knew just what to do.

In this, his private spa, Ryan could be seen practicing Yoga, or so it seemed. The muscles and tendons of his fast-growing legs needed to be frequently stretched in order to be able to carry more of his increasing body weight.

We made Ryan's world as amenable as we could—considering he couldn't be free in the wild. He was given a bucket of water for drinking and after splashing around in his new pool, he would hop out, shake off, and dry. Surely, the only thing missing was a masseuse and some raw carrot juice!

This particular Yoga pose is otherwise known as the Warrior I or Virabhadrasana pose.

Photo by Kathy Campbell

I Can Fly!

"Never abandon your vision. Keep reaching to further your dreams."

Benjamin Banneker, African-American almanac author, surveyor, landowner and farmer

One person with a particularly soft heart for Ryan Gosling initially placed pans of water in the quad for him and his family. As he grew, she would seek him out in the quiet of evening each week and especially when he seemed to go missing. She would look along the walls and behind the trees and bushes and was always relieved when she'd find him. Often, when he was simply chilling in his pool, she'd have a heart-to-heart conversation with him that went something like this: "Now listen little fella, this has gone on long enough. You need to learn to fly."

While he lacked guidance from Mother Goose, Ryan got help from Mother Nature. Amazingly, Ryan taught himself to fly! It was completely instinctive and mesmerizing. He would run from one end of the quad to the other gaining speed, and eventually our little boy would become airborne for a few seconds. When he realized he could fly it seemed to "freak him out." It made me think of Peter Pan's song, "You can fly, you can fly, you can fly!!!" Oh, what a big beautiful boy he was turning out to be! And yes, he could fly, but never away.

Eyas in Need

<hr />

"No act of kindness, no matter how small, is ever wasted."

Aesop, ancient Greek storyteller

Meanwhile, on the outside of the building, another family was growing up. Cooper's hawks live as long as 12 or more years. Like the geese, they are monogamous, but do not always mate for life. It's actually the male who builds the nest with occasional help from the female. We could see that nest on the other side of the quad through our office windows. It was well below the top of a tree and looked like a pile of sticks, but we learned that sometimes bark flakes and green twigs are used. Several people saw them on their side of the building and once watched one hawk almost fly into the window! Some paper was taped to the window to discourage a near collision from happening again.

These hawk parents had two eyas (ah'-yes), chicks or hatchlings. We know because one day they desperately needed to be rescued. One was on a branch below the nest and by midday, the two were on the ground, but were not well. They looked to be about 12 inches and were dehydrated, but squawking showing that they still had some energy. In a dangerous heat wave, the temperature climbed to 109 degrees. Two kindly gentleman from the office placed them in a box and drove them to the Wildlife Care Association* at the old McClellan Air Force Base, now McClellan Business Park. From there, the volunteers transported the pair to the California Raptor Center,* which is a part of the UC Davis School of Veterinary Medicine. I couldn't help thinking that the mama and papa hawks must have been devastated to be missing their offspring. We were told after rehabilitation that the eyas would be released back into the same area where they were rescued, so we may yet see them again. I might add that the two rescuers were issued a "red star" commendation from the company Chief Operating Officer.

SEE RESOURCES SECTION

Rumor Has It or the Great Escape!!!

———◦———

"I'll not budge an inch."

William Shakespeare, English playwright, poet, and actor

He's gone! What do you mean, "He's gone!?" Little Ryan has flown the coop! The nice folks who provided the kiddie pool, water bucket, and goose feed removed said accommodations to encourage Ryan Gosling to start a new chapter in his life. As fate would have it, one day we saw a large gaggle of geese (a group of geese on the ground) on the other side of the building, away from the quad. There were about two dozen lounging in the shade on the grass. It was a lovely sight. I saw the geese as I was leaving for lunch and hoped that just maybe, Ryan could meet them. When I returned they were gone and Ryan was still alone.

On the following Monday, a story began swirling. There was a rumor that Ryan went off with other geese. Could it be so? I went across the quad to speak with the people from the other company who, like us, were watching daily from their respective windows. They too saw the Canada geese activities unfold from the beginning and I wanted to know if they had more stories to tell. They mostly saw what we saw, but the funniest thing about our parallel universes was that we had both named the baby, Ryan Gosling! We laughed at that.

I also found out that one lady with an office facing the quad had to chase the hawk away many more times than I realized. She could see the hawk's shadow while it was perching and when she did, she tore into the quad to help the geese by shooing the hawk away. The challenge was that the gosling would always waddle just a bit too far away from one of the parents. I'm almost glad I didn't know how often this happened, as I was worried enough for the baby.

Finally, I learned the details about Ryan's departure. It seems that two of the staff had come in on the weekend to wash the swimming pool, which was on the south end of the quad. There, you can see through the glass to the other side of the building on the side where the hawks made their nest. Lo and behold, a much smaller family of geese than we had previously seen, were lounging. Just a mom and six babies; no dad was evident and it was thought that he was scouting. The babies were not really little. In fact, it was estimated that they were only about one week younger than Ryan Gosling.

On a snap decision, one of the people simply opened a quad door and tried to escort Ryan through the building to meet up with this new family. We could have always let Ryan out the door to freedom through the breezeway that connected the two companies, but that was a frightening prospect, forbidden due to the proximity to the hawk's nest. Keeping him safe in his "nursery" seemed wise at the time. Either way, escorting Ryan through the building at this wonderfully opportune moment was not going to be easy.

First, the mom and teens decided it was time to leave. Off they went. One of the people quickly went to herd them back, but it was a "wild goose chase!" Then, they had to deal with the Little King. They managed to get Ryan through the first set of breezeway doors, but he was not convinced. No sir. Each time he was walked forward, Ryan spun around and flew back over their heads to his nursery and the people had to start all over again. If only he could see the mom and her teens, but he didn't. This went on for a half a dozen times until Ryan finally saw the family, who had returned, complaining all the way, and charged forward with a great deal of excitement to greet them at last. Eureka!

As it turned out, the teens protested. Mom, however, instantly sized up the youngster and accepted him into her brood as if this was the most natural of all things. They waddled off into the sunset with a new member of their family, and Ryan left his human family behind. We knew this surrogate Mom would lovingly teach him the rest of his lessons and Ryan would never be alone again.

It was the best possible ending.

Here's Where Our Story Ends... or Does It?

"Hope is the thing with feathers—that perches in the soul..."

Emily Elizabeth Dickinson, American poet

In our reading about geese, we learned that the parents will always return to the exact site of the previous year's nest in March, April, or May and the offspring will return close to where they were born.

Does that mean we will see Ryan Gosling and his parents around the same time, same place next year? Only time will tell. We know the trials and tribulations of raising a gosling in the courtyard, so it would not be best, but I have to confess, and I suspect others feel the same, we hope to see them again.

EPILOGUE

We have since seen dozens of geese nearby on the hill opposite our facility, but roadwork is now in progress. It seems that the city is widening a thoroughfare with the added intention of connecting it to another road. Growth in the community is constant and habitat for the animals is dwindling. Thankfully, the geese can fly and there is a nearby golf course and lake where they are still welcome.

We can only hope that Ryan Gosling eventually found his parents within the gaggle and that it was a happy reunion. We know that they can recognize their family members, amazing creatures that they are. We wish them all well and particularly that Ryan, the Little King, is ever safely shielded within the flock and off living his life to the fullest.

PART 2

Year Two

The Return of the Geese

The Return of the Canada Geese

———◦———

"Can't repeat the past?…Why of course you can!"

F. Scott Fitzgerald, American novelist and screenwriter

February 2

We had been awaiting our guests. Then we saw them. First, a single pair of Canada geese flew into the courtyard and sauntered about, but we couldn't tell if they were last year's mated couple. Then we noticed a second set of geese fly in and then out…along with the occasional hawk. Who were they? Every day we peered outside from a long, enclosed, glass corridor stretching the length of the courtyard. In fishbowl-style, we watched and wondered if a pair of geese would remain. I continually asked staff if they saw any nesting activity as one person might see what another might not during the course of a workday.

A Goose is Nesting!

"Tis a light pang. I like to see the nests still in their places..."
Edward Thomas, British Poet

April 2

I finally saw her today! A Canada goose. You could see her head peeking out atop the roof of the courtyard's southern rest area right outside our office door. It was the "sister" rest area on top of which the geese built a nest last year at the far north side. There was no question that seeing her planted there meant nesting had begun.

A large branch hung over the nest of eggs, providing a sense of protection from the resident hawk. Last year the goose did not have such a shield, which had devastating results with only one goose egg surviving after the others were attacked, broken, and scattered across the ground. The singular egg would eventually hatch, bestowing its precious charge to the world, the Gosling Ryan.

This year's nest seemed unscathed with no broken eggs. With my vacation plans nearing, I hoped that the goslings would not hatch until I returned on Monday, April 30, but nature will do what nature wants. It takes 30 days for Canada goose eggs to hatch, and she had already been up there for at least a week. I fretted that I would likely not witness the first gosling milestones.

From the roof

Who are You?

"The best mirror is an old friend."

George Herbert, Welsh-born poet, orator

If I could only see the goose more clearly, I might be able to confirm if this goose was indeed Mother Goose, the name we gave to last year's female of the mated pair. Some felt confident that the Gosling Ryan brought a mate back and it was they who returned to nest. However, research confirmed that a gosling will not fully mature and nest for three years though they may start to find a mate earlier. Of course, the Gosling Ryan could have been "Rihanna," the alternative name we thought of calling the baby, as we did not know if last year's gosling was a male or female. Either way, it was two years too soon for the offspring to return.

I knew I had to get up on the roof for a better view of the nest, so I secured permission to enter a restricted door, through a narrow area, and up a fixed ladder to the roof. I held tightly onto a couple of handrails and carefully ascended. Once on the roof, I walked around, looking beyond the building, viewing the landscape from a grand perspective that I had never seen before, but that was only a preview. I purposefully took my time to build up my excitement for the main event for which I was not going to be disappointed.

I finally headed to the courtyard side of the roof and looked down—and there she was, a nesting Canada goose, of the largest species of geese in the world. She was breathtaking.

It was an overcast day and it had just finished raining. The tree leaves were a deep green made darker by the rain. The mood was both tranquil and reverent. I was in photography heaven snapping away, and I couldn't wait to review the photos as I desperately wanted to identify her.

Far from being an ornithologist, I nevertheless conducted research and learned that indeed, after the female lays the eggs, it is she who sits on them. Since only the female nests, determining some of her notable physical features would help distinguish her from her mate.

From the roof, I scanned the courtyard looking for the gander. He was nowhere in sight. We named last year's mate, Hawkeye, who steadfastly protected his little family. I knew that if the female was Mother Goose, then with certainty, the gander would have to be him.

Designed to choose a mate for a lifetime commitment, a mated pair can appear romantic with intricate greeting displays – as if they were in love! Anthropomorphizing is something humans do to describe pets and other animals in human terms, and it's no wonder I did. If

you were to have seen the geese in action, you might, too. Consider that they only mate once per year. That means for the rest of the time they stay close, with the gander clearly murmuring, cooing, and hovering over the female with great care and contentment until they have their goslings, at which time they both focus on and share the parenting.

One could argue that the courtyard is, in fact, an adequate place to make a nest and raise a family. Yet, as we learned 12 months earlier when tragedy befell last year's goslings, it is not ideal. Either way, we knew the male would return soon, as his mate needed him on patrol.

The picture of the nesting goose, taken from the roof, was the last one I took before my vacation. I planned to research how to identify geese and study the photos after my return. I was uncertain what I would discover. In the meantime, I asked my colleagues to share their photos in my absence should the big day occur while I was gone.

There was one thing that I was certain of—now that the parents were expecting, the buzz about our guests would escalate.

PHOTO BY LAURIE HENRY

56

The Hawk Report—an Update on "Eyas in Need"

"The hawk is aerial brother of the wave which he sails over..."

Henry David Thoreau, American naturalist, essayist, poet, and philosopher

I received a thank you card from the California Raptor Center (CRC) yesterday. I had paid it forward, donating future profits to them from a previous edition of this book that I also signed and sent along. Jo Cowen, the center's education coordinator since 1992, wrote back that she and her staff were grateful for the funds and told me that they were all enjoying the book. She added the best news of all...our two eyas (baby hawks) survived! (See Part 1—Year One, *Along Came Ryan, the Little Gosling King*, Chapter, "Eyas in Need.")

On average, the CRC rescues 300 hawks in a year, but during the course of the heat wave last year, which lasted one week and reached 109 degrees—dangerous for every living creature including humans— they rescued 40 hawks! Of those 40, two were eyas rescued by Quest's staff. The two babies were the offspring of our resident, spotted Cooper's hawk. They had become dehydrated and fallen out of their nest just on the other side of the courtyard wall (not in the courtyard itself.) The CRC said that all but one of the 40 hawks were rehabilitated and released back into their respective communities. That one is still at the center— they didn't say if the hawk will be released later or is now a permanent guest, as sometimes happens.

As much as we were in awe of the hawks, we worried for the geese. Just the other day, I saw four hawks soaring elegantly, yet ominously, over the soccer field-sized courtyard. They were riding high on air currents, but we knew any goslings that hatched would be prime targets and the geese parents would be vigilantly standing guard.

Hawks soaring over courtyard

Roseville, California

---○---

"The oak it is a noble tree, the monarch of the wood; through winter's storms a thousand years, its hardy trunk hath stood."

Ann Hawkshaw, English poet

April 23

Roseville, California is located at the base of the foothills leading to Tahoe National Forest with snow-capped winter mountains clearly visible in the distance. It is considered a Mediterranean climate with distinct seasons of cool wet winters, hot summers, gorgeous springs, and deeply-colored, rich autumns.

In the late 1800s, Roseville was a stagecoach station, a settlement called Griders. By the early 1900s, a period of expansion took place, and the burgeoning town boasted the largest ice manufacturing plant in the world (Pacific Fruit Express Building, in 1913). Roseville went on to become a railroad town for decades until air travel and the national Interstate Highway System forced the railroad into decline. While the railroad is still a major employer, the city started to boom attracting diverse businesses.

Roseville is also bountiful. Long before railroads or the town itself, there were vast grasslands filled with lush flora and fauna and gloriously thick groves of valley oaks. Wolves, grizzly bears, cougars, elk, deer, eagles, hawks, and geese were among the wild animals that shared in the land's wealth.

The geese are actually only part-time visitors, but from time immemorial a huge array of waterfowl, including nearly a million geese, migrate each year along the Northern California flyway that passes over Roseville.

The area also attracted one of the most famous tribes of Native American Indians: the Maidu, who were hunter-gatherers and fishers and are widely celebrated in the region.

To this day, Roseville still maintains its charm as a desirable place for people...and Canada geese.

Maidu Coiled Basket, Mary Kea'a'ala Azbill Maidu, Native American, 1864-1932

Mazel Tov

"Nature is painting for us, day after day, pictures of infinite beauty if only we have the eyes to see them."

John Ruskin, English Art Critic, watercolorist and philanthropist

April 23

Roseville also enjoys stunning skies with a spectacle of clouds against vivid blue. Such was the case this day....

A pink streak appeared in the east and light shone, slanting through the trees. As it grew lighter, the shadows grew in front of a pair of proud Canada geese and their five goslings. It was the dawn of a new day and five new lives, but I was away and unable to witness the sight first-hand. I received several urgent messages with photos from two Canada goose fans displaying the newly hatched babies. I felt like a proud aunt.

As we learned last year, downy goslings can flutter off a low roof to the ground without injury. While no one reported seeing this darling, dare-devil scene, we knew that's how they landed onto the courtyard.

I had a whole week before I was to return and meet "the kids." I summoned patience, but was anxious to get home. In fact, I don't ever remember looking forward more to going to work on a Monday as I did then.

Photo by Sarah B Fox

65

Then There Were Four—Rainbow, River, Ridge, And Rebel

"One bird went over the blue sky
It's blue as far as you can see.
Nobody knows what's behind the sky.
He went over the sky
Just to show the others what he could do."

Maidu Tribal song

May 4

Too quickly, we counted only four babies when there had been five. It was heartbreaking, but we understand the harsh realities of nature. The parents must have put up a fight as we know they did last year when they were able to save their baby, the Gosling Ryan, from being taken by the resident hawk. With four remaining goslings to raise, there was no place for extended grieving in their world.

It was also about time that the goslings were given names.

In honor of the Gosling Ryan, the namesake of the first year's story, I called his siblings, Rainbow, River, Ridge, and Rebel.

Rebel is injured

Trouble Finds Rebel

"Adopt the pace of nature: her secret is patience."

Ralph Waldo Emerson, American essayist, philosopher, poet

May 7

One of the goslings, the "rebel" of the bunch, suddenly went lame. We thought we would lose him because he was struggling to move forward, and when he did, he propelled himself on his little stomach. We painfully watched and tried to imagine what chance he had against a hawk in this condition. Still, the family stayed near him. They refused to abandon their little Rebel—never leaving him alone. We were able to get fairly close, but with the parent's threatening warnings, we decided it would be best to wait a day before we seriously considered intervening.

By now, I was visiting the geese in the courtyard twice a day and observed that they would occasionally hiss at me if I neared the "no go zone"—the respected personal space between us. When getting too close, imprinting can become a serious matter, as wild animals, especially geese, can get accustomed to people. Goslings are well-known to imprint on anyone, including friendly dogs, and then comically follow them around.

Watching the geese had been an extraordinary pleasure up to this time, but this turn of events was extraordinarily heart-wrenching. By evening, Rebel had crossed the courtyard and we observed him lifting himself up, limping, falling, trying again, and having a tough time keeping up with his parents and siblings.

Nature, however, can be amazingly charitable. So it was with Rebel.

The next day, and quite surprisingly, Rebel was staying upright, moving quickly with only the slightest limp and the word "miracle" was whispered throughout the company with sighs of relief. Upon reflection, we realized that babies grow fast and can heal even faster. We just needed to be cautiously patient and when all was said and done, we were just happy that nature was astonishingly kind, this time.

Still, we wondered what could have caused Rebel's lameness. I have read that ganders can sometimes attack goslings, but they are less likely to attack their own, and we had never seen this gander show signs of aggression toward his offspring. On the other hand, it could have been a turkey who might have flown into the courtyard or possibly one of the alien geese who made an appearance. A pair of foreign geese did fly in, and they occasionally fought with our resident geese in tremendous skirmishes. With the babies underfoot, it occurred to us that Rebel could have been injured in just such a scenario.

John viewing the family

Rebel trying to keep up

Invaders

"Upon the conduct of each depends the fate of all."

Alexander the Great, Macedonian king and legendary leader

In the end, the parents did not chase the invading geese away. Living for a while in a truce, they managed instead to hash out their territorial differences. We would see them all communing together, just "being," albeit the two groups maintained a healthy distance. While the parents occasionally hounded the invaders, it was now done half-heartedly. I did, however, see one walking around with a suspicious looking feather in its mouth and one feather partly pulled out of its neck.

Perhaps the other set of geese had their babies snatched in some distant nesting area and they had nothing better to do than socialize in the courtyard. They could have used last year's abandoned courtyard nest, but these aliens showed no attempt at nesting and it was rather late in the season to do so anyhow. All this hypothesizing aside, the most likely reason for their extended stay was because the neighboring business had put out some grain to supplement the resident geese's limited menu of grass and shrubbery—enough for all. Either way, I liked their presence because an extra pair of geese would help keep the hawks at bay.

Two weeks later the invaders flew off for good. They might have been frightened when the maintenance team began a regimen of hosing down the courtyard walkways. Our resident geese were used to that routine. Besides, they were not going anywhere while their babies still needed constant attention, schooling, and protection.

Parade of the Geese

Abbey Road, Take II

Forward march

Left right left right

To the rear march

Left face

About turn

Eyes left

Right face

Double time

Stand at ease

Fall out

Home inspection

The Mystery House

"...those who have wealth must here and now do good deeds that will live for a long time."

Thiruvalluvar, Tamil, India Poet and philosopher

May 8

Out of kindness, someone at Cokeva, the adjoining business, constructed a beautiful little goose house on the other side of the courtyard—a good deed praised by all. The house was plainly built to draw the geese inside of it, thereby providing shelter from the hawk after the terrible loss of one gosling. No one reported seeing the geese use it, though a few assorted smaller birds greedily helped themselves to the bounty of grain placed within. Either way, the house was a charming surprise.

A little research shed light on goose houses—only domestic geese will use them. In nature at night, wild geese sleep in the water, taking "sentinel" shifts. The water offers them added protection from predators that might enter the water and arouse the geese with warning ripples, while other marauders might splash noisily and expose their presence. This, of course, was a non-issue in the courtyard as there is no body of water.

Still, the mystery house was not built in vain. In fact, the geese thoroughly enjoyed congregating around it daily. It didn't hurt that their main source of water from an outdoor spigot was next to the house along with a pan filled with a generous allowance of grain. The water flowed constantly and gently from a hose into a low pan as their special "water cooler."

We would often find both the babies and the parents drinking or floating around throughout their stay. We had already learned last year that feeding the wild geese would not thwart their normal activities, though there is contradiction to be found. Ideally, and under normal circumstances, wild animals should not be fed because they can become dependent on humans and it may disrupt breeding, as more offspring than normal may be born or hatched, causing a multitude of other issues.

It would be two months before the "mystery" of the mystery house was to be solved, but for now....

Round or pointed tail?

Body of Evidence

"Happiness is being with an old friend after a long time and feeling like nothing has changed."

Anonymous

I finally began to compare all the photos of the Canada goose parents from the year before to this year; I realized it was going to be a big job. It seemed I first had to identify which was the male and which was the female.

I had a few basic facts. I've read that you can distinguish them by their tail shape, but doing so eluded me. What was indicated is that the round tail would be identified with the male and the pointed tail, the female, but what is considered round and what is pointed? They both looked so similar and my eyes glazed over comparing dozens of goose tail photos.

I've also read that with careful observation you can differentiate between male and female geese by their vocal sounds. However, with 13 different calls, including clucks, murmurs, and honking, I'm afraid that was a bit too much studying for the time I had visiting with them.

I learned that males and females have other distinguishing characteristics as well. Females have a somewhat pointed bill, slimmer, shorter necks than males, and their head crowns are generally smaller and narrower. It was equally challenging to identify them with these features, though.

Demure Mother Goose smooth neckline

Ducks, the Canada goose's migratory brethren, are much easier to tell apart. That is, the male has a distinctly curled feathered tail and the female doesn't. The male also has brilliant iridescent-colored feathers and the female has bland, brown feathers—at least for the wild ducks.

It was not going to be as easy to identify the gender of our geese with certainty… a veterinarian would need to examine the birds.

Then there's a weight differential. On average, the male Canada goose can be two pounds heavier than the female; 14 pounds versus approximately 12. That seemed to help when the parent geese were close enough together to compare, but you needed a particularly sharp eye with only a two-pound differential in weight.

All this is fine and good when trying to tell the male from the female, but the $64,000 question was: Are these the same mated Canada geese as those that visited last year? Short of tagging the geese, which I wouldn't, couldn't, and didn't do, I simply would not be able to know.

I felt sure that the key was in the nesting photos. I knew already the nesting goose was the female, but as I zoomed in to all of her features on the photo images, the one trait I neglected to think about was her chinstrap, which is a white band or patch on a Canada goose's cheek that runs under its chin like a strap. Chinstraps vary and can have slender, wide, or oblong patterns. They are, in fact, unique identifying attributes like a human iris or fingerprint. From my vantage point on the roof and when I first saw her while standing in the courtyard and looking up, I could clearly see both left and right sides of her profile and thus her chinstrap.

With close examination, I was fairly certain that I could identify the same chinstrap when I saw it with my bare eyes. I knew though that I would have to pour over the photos or get close enough to the geese in the courtyard in order to do so. And did I mention the chinstraps are also uniquely different from one side of the head to the other?

Even with this added complexity, it didn't take me long. Photo after photo from the year before versus the new ones the following year pointed to only one

Hawkeye's widow's peak

undeniable conclusion. The nesting goose was indeed Mother Goose! And that meant the gander had to be Hawkeye.

In the process of my intense chinstrap scrutiny, I picked up on another profiling feature, the neckline. Hawkeye had a beautiful widow's peak neckline that was highly visible looking at him straight on. It was a fluid curve of black ending in a point in the middle. Mother Goose had a perfectly clean, curved line gracing her neck. I soon became more comfortable identifying them and began to see their different facial expressions, and could even see some similarities between the young ones and their parents—not unlike humans and most animals. I felt immensely relieved and satisfied, like I had cracked a mysterious code—and indeed I finally had. With all of this body of evidence, the verdict was in and the case was now closed.

Feathers dangling off and around

Molting and Landlocked

"What man-made machine will ever achieve the complete perfection of even the goose's wing?"

Abbas ibn Firnas, Andalusian polymath: an inventor, physician, chemist

June 11

Rainbow, River, Ridge, and Rebel grew rapidly. They began to develop their own unique chinstraps. Their bodies were not quite as tall or as brown as their parents, their necks were still a little gray rather than the sleek black of adult Canada geese, and they had not completely lost the baby tuft atop their heads. In an affectionate way, they were still babies to me. In reality, they were technically "juveniles" who started growing their young, shiny tail feathers to allow them to fly.

The parents, on the other hand, were losing theirs! A profuse number of feathers appeared all over the quad. Having learned about molting from the previous year, we knew that the Canada goose parents had begun to molt.

The molting season caused anxiety with the staff because when geese lose their feathers they cannot fly at all. By this time last year, the parents had been taking off and periodically returning before their permanent departure when they abandoned the Gosling Ryan and sent us all into a frenzy. We worried that would be their mode again, and we presumed that they knew they would be stuck for a long time if they did not leave while they still could fly. It appeared these two had made up their minds; they were rooted.

I photographed the feathers that you could often see dangling off of the parents' tails or scattered about the grounds. The feathers were clearly worn and ragged from their flights to distant areas and you could see why they needed to be completely replaced–like tires on a car.

When the parents had lost nearly all of their flying feathers, I didn't take notice at first. Carefully viewing photos of them, I kept going back to one in particular and thought how unfortunate that there was a glare reflecting back from the window through which I was photographing them that day. To my horror, after blowing the photo up, I realized it was not a glare at all but an area entirely devoid of feathers, leaving only shiny bones! The molting of the feathers exposed the wing skeleton—a shocking sight. These thin and hollow bones reminded me of a Halloween skeleton costume. Both wings molt at the same time and with these primary feathers gone, geese are rendered completely flightless for three to six weeks.

Other types of birds do not lose their flight feathers in the same fashion. Instead, they lose and replace one feather at a time, so they never become flightless.

Rebel

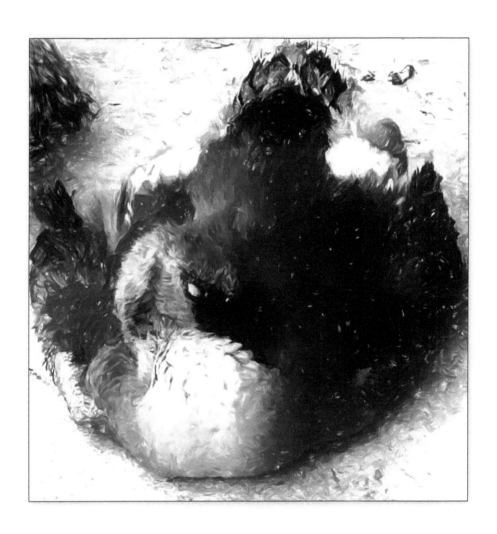

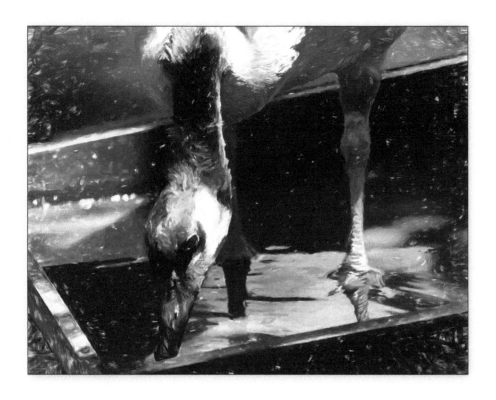

Rainbow (left) and Rebel (right)

Photo by Arutro Sandoval

Mother Goose and Rainbow

School's in Session

<hr/>

"Education is not preparation for life; education is life itself."

John Dewey, American philosopher, psychologist, and educational reformer

June 14

The clockwork timing of nature doesn't cease. When the goslings are seven to ten weeks old, they are capable of sustained flight and are essentially "full-grown." To get them prepared, the mated pair flung open the school doors and began to hold classes. You'd see the parents take off running, flapping their wings, while the juveniles followed suit running as fast as their little webbed feet could take them, and flapping their own much smaller wings. And then they'd do it again, and again, and again with strict repetition, not unlike Mr. Miyagi's martial arts instruction in *The Karate Kid*—"Wax on, wax off."

As to swimming, that came naturally, but no one placed a kiddie pool out in the courtyard this year as they had done the year before for the Gosling Ryan and his parents. Next to the dangers of a resident hawk, not having a body of water in this nesting place has to be the second biggest drawback for them as we learned that goslings expertly swim and dive 25 feet within 24 hours of hatching. They are waterfowl after all.

It is a guess, but a reasonable one, that with four goslings, they would have demolished one of those kiddie pools in short order. The Gosling Ryan did just that to his first plastic pool, but a second, sturdier one prevailed. A nearly indestructible pool would have been needed for Rainbow, River, Ridge, and Rebel—maybe one made of steel.

Splish Splash

"Animals are such agreeable friends — they ask no questions, they pass no criticisms."

George Eliot, English novelist, essayist and translator

June 18

No one got more excited than the gosling Rainbow when the lawn's in-ground sprinkler irrigation system automatically started. The sprinkler heads popped up like a jack-in-the-box at a designated daily time, providing complete coverage as they cycled their way through the grounds.

It seemed Rainbow became accustomed to the timing of the spouts, spreading her wings and clamoring to the "water park" with Dad in the lead and her siblings and Mom in the rear. The sprinklers methodically rotated in overlapping succession, which the geese followed like the Pied Piper. They were splashing, drinking, honking, and running around with abandon like kids playing around a gushing New York City fire hydrant that was mischievously loosed on the street. We didn't know who was more delighted, all of us watching the show or the little Canada goose family. I think it was a tie, but after watching Rainbow splishin' and splashin' underneath the sprinkler-created rainbow, it was clear that she and the rest of the gaggle were having the time of their lives.

PHOTO BY VIVIAN AEDO

Blackbird—a vocal visitor

All-Points Bulletin: Goslings Gone

"*The pain passes, but the beauty remains.*"

Pierre-Auguste Renoir, French impressionist painter

I was doing my usual lunch rounds, checking in with the little goose family and saw them lounging under a shady bush, staying cool in the heat of summer. Then black birds, who recently showed up, started squawking and dive bombing. Disturbed, the geese got up and began moving along the building perimeter. I thought nothing of it at first. When I walked over to photograph them next to one of the glass windows, I could see the geese's reflection. The reflection tricked my mind into thinking that they were all there, but upon closer inspection, I saw only two goslings and my heart raced.

By now the young ones looked nearly as big as their parents, but close up, they still had fuzzy crowns and baby faces, so I frantically started to count, pointing like a child at the moving creatures. I counted again as my brain and eyes compared notes. My heart was in denial and in those seconds, I thought that I was counting wrong. Coming to my senses, I began combing the courtyard around the trees, bushes, and small hiding places, but to no avail.

As in the five stages of grief and loss, I went from denial to anger, who did what—the hawk, a person? I could feel gloom lurking. Finally, in an agonizing moment, I accepted that two goslings were gone!

I commiserated with several staff including Kathy, one of the chief advocates for our Canada goose family for the last two years. She said she would send feelers out to investigate the disappearance.

Kathy was known to commune with the Gosling Ryan in the evenings before she went home and contributed two photos of him including the one where he's floating in his plastic kiddie pool.

In the end, no one saw or knew what happened, but some say people were trying to get the Canada goose family to fly away intact, but only succeeded in getting two out of the courtyard. I lost sleep over it, wondering how the two were going to make it on their own and if they were somehow still together. The juveniles, now capable of flight, would ordinarily stay with their parents for a year and follow them during their first migration in advance of finding other young geese to form or join groups. In this courtyard environment though, nothing was ordinary.

By now, I realized I was going to write Part 2—Year Two: *The Return of the Geese,* but what should I write about this episode? I longed for a happy ending.

I continued to dig for facts and noticed that when I visited the remaining geese they appeared uptight and even ran from me. These are social and friendly animals so it was perplexing. It lent credence to the human's efforts to get them to fly away.

Within a day or so, however, the geese seemed to relax as animals often do. Still, I was heartbroken for the young ones, so I decided to press people at the other business, but most knew nothing. Cokeva's HR Manager, Lisa, promised to have their maintenance manager contact me and share information he might have.

Regardless, these young Canada geese are nothing but punctual. They were hatched on April 23 and the two left on June 27, exactly 8½ weeks later, right about when they are supposed to be able to fly.

The day two goslings flew out

Uptight

Mother Goose and Hawkeye—Alone

"Until one has loved an animal, a part of one's soul remains unawakened."

Anatole France, French poet, journalist, and novelist

Two weeks later, the last two babies flew out and the parents were alone. I had already researched and knew that though the parents were molting, losing their tattered and old flying feathers from their 5,000 mile migration, they could fly again in four to six weeks when their new feathers finished growing back. I checked my notes and we were getting close if not already at that point. Last year the parents took off and abandoned the Gosling Ryan just before they completely molted. In retrospect, we believe they knew their offspring was finished with his lessons and could survive on his own. In addition, we considered that this year, the parents had a bigger job with more babies to care for, so perhaps that is why they remained through the molting season.

I didn't mind if Mother Goose and Hawkeye left, too, because if their babies were nearby, the family might be reunited as they have an amazing ability to identify each other! That offered me hope. Indeed, I had heard of sightings of one or two of the juveniles in the general vicinity of our data center.

With all the babies gone, the parents looked terribly forlorn, if not exhausted. They seemed to mope near each other for hours, getting up periodically to feed. For someone who had observed them for over five months, it is not hard to believe the veracity of these observations.

I did not know what to expect next—I should have.

Mother Goose and Hawkeye, tired and forlorn

Hawkeye

Mom

Dad

Empty courtyard

Like the Phoenix

"The Phoinix (Phoenix) knows how to reckon...without the aid of arithmetic, for it is a pupil of all-wise nature..."

Aelian, Greek writer, second century A.D.

July 12, 10:00 AM

The very next morning, we discovered they too were gone. Like a phoenix rising from the ashes, the Canada geese, with their new flying feathers fully functional, rose up to the sky and away.

One Last Goodbye

"Good night, good night! Parting is such sweet sorrow."

Romeo and Juliet, William Shakespeare, English playwright, poet, and actor

July 12, 11:30 AM

Later that morning, Kathy excitedly announced that there was a pair of geese in front of Quest's building! I ran outside to see if it was our mated pair and indeed it was. I discovered Mother Goose and Hawkeye relaxing on the grass under a very tall tree, no longer imprisoned by four walls, but instead, free at last, appearing refreshed and transformed—always the Zen masters.

With Mother Goose and Hawkeye's final appearance, it seemed as if they were saying goodbye.... and, it was a fitting goodbye. I was grateful to have had the chance to see them one last time and bid my friends adieu.

Family Album

Hawkeye on patrol

Shady characters

Photo by Arutro Sandoval

La Casita

"It is good people that make good places."

Anna Sewell, English novelist, author of *Black Beauty*

I photographed the geese for the final time this year in front of our building. I then made one last visit into the courtyard to see if any of the juveniles might have flown back in—wishful thinking—but none had.

After strolling around the quad, soaking in the emptiness, it was time to head back toward Quest's offices. Just then, a gentleman, who had been sitting on a bench and who I had never seen before, called to me. He said he had seen me taking pictures before. We introduced ourselves and I was elated to meet him. It was Arturo Sandoval, Cokeva's Maintenance Manager.

All along I had been hearing Arturo's name in relation to the geese. After all, the courtyard's care was his responsibility. We sat through lunch and breathlessly shared photos, videos, and stories of our mutual feathered friends, including those from the year before.

Arturo said that the geese had been his passion and a sort of "therapy" for the last two years. He said he spoke Spanish to the Gosling Ryan when he previously inhabited the courtyard, and affectionately referred to him as his "grandson." I was taken aback that he thought this year's gander was the Gosling Ryan. Considering how much investigatory research I had done, it makes sense that few people would know the identity of the geese. When I let him know that they were the same mated pair who nested last year, he was truly surprised and maybe just a little disappointed, but as a man in touch with nature, he recognized, how wonderful this truly was. I further shared that if the Gosling Ryan returns, he will not do so for a couple more years and only if the Gosling Ryan was actually "Rihanna," a female. If the Gosling Ryan was a male, in time, he would find his own mate and the two would likely nest at her brooding area.

I inquired about the Mystery House. With a big smile, Arturo said he built it. He christened it "La Casita"—a very good name. Arturo confirmed what we guessed at all along...that he was compelled to construct it after we lost one of the goslings to the hawk. I thanked him for his efforts and let him know that many people in the business across the way where I work were delighted and impressed by the beautiful "little house"—La Casita.

Arturo told me that there were mixed feelings about having the geese in the courtyard where Cokeva staff strolled during their breaks, and after discussing the situation with Cokeva CEO, Ann Nguyen, she gave her blessing to both welcome and keep the geese protected. They are, Arturo encouraged, a lucky and powerful symbol of abundance.

Arturo also shared that there were two women on his maintenance team, Rosita and Yanitzin, who were dedicated to the immaculate care of the courtyard. They had impressive professional tools, including a high pressure, heavy-duty power washer—perfect for the huge job at hand. Even so, Quest people helped once or twice. Debra and Sarah found some shovels and tidied up a bit more near Quest's doors as we'd found that geese can rapidly transform their home into unpleasant grounds for people to walk around. Considering there were six of them, well... you get the picture.

This was a good day on so many levels, particularly in meeting Arturo, who was not just a fan of the geese, but my missing link; he took care of the geese and I chronicled and memorialized them in photos and verse.

Arturo at work

140

Yanitzen and Rosita

Debra (foreground) and Sarah

Emptiness and Ennui

"Remembrance and reflection how allied! What thin partitions sense
from thought divide!"

Alexander Pope, eighteenth century English poet

July 12, 6:00 PM

After my workday, I stood alone in the empty courtyard reflecting on the geese and this second year of their visit. With their life force missing, one thought rose up, that while goslings come and goslings go, the mated pair was committed to one another above all else. Together, the beating heart of their existence was to raise, nurture, and send their babies off to live their lives — and that is exactly what they did.

With their job done and their presence departed, a palpable lull enveloped me.

Epilogue—Until We Meet Again

"Each time you see that indelible V-formation, be grateful for the perfect moment to be alive. And should you hear the geese calling, drink it in, knowing that you have been touched with the indescribable magnificence of the Canada geese."

Barbara Klide, American author

July 13

Since the female of the Canada geese are "philopatric" or likely to return to the same breeding area each year, I became filled with hope if not expectation. I cannot confidently say that is what Mother Goose will do, but if she does return, I will be able to recognize her. And you can bet Hawkeye will be right there with her.

Mother Goose and Hawkeye had a good run for a second year in a row at this place of business. Except for one, their babies thrived, and so they may return to the courtyard again. We will excitedly hope and wait for them and if they do honor us with yet a third visit, we will joyously celebrate the return of the geese.

Strike a Pose

Mother Goose and Hawkeye

Mother Goose and Hawkeye

Hawkeye and Mother Goose

Mother Goose

Hawkeye

Hawkeye

Mother Goose

Mother Goose

Mother Goose

Hawkeye

Mother Goose

Hawkeye and Mother Goose

Fall in the courtyard

Musings and After Stories from the Courtyard

Rabbits and Lizards and Opossoms! Oh, my!

"One should pay attention to even the smallest crawling creature for these too may have a valuable lessons to teach us."

Heȟáka Sápa, known as Black Elk, Oglala Lakota Sioux holy man, warrior, survivor

July 19

There is a great deal of animal life around the Quest data center besides geese and hawks—all manner of little furry, scary, scaly, and flying animals and insects make their home there. We often see jackrabbits skitter across the vast lawn in front of our facility; sometimes two or three are seen in the early morning or early evening. They are preyed upon by the hawks. Someone reported seeing a hawk swooping down towards a rabbit just the other day, but the lucky rabbit made it safely under bushes near some trees. It was an undeniably close call.

We also see many lizards. I don't have a clue about which variety they are and with 45 species of them in California, I'll let someone else write that book. I have noticed, though, that many of them have dazzling lizard skin, especially in direct sunlight when it appears iridescent. Since lizards are known to eat pest insects, they are welcome.

The opossum surprised us all. I had seen a furry creature out of the corner of my eye from inside my office window. Thinking it was a cat, when I turned to get a good look, I was mightily surprised. This little fellow seemed to be a healthy young one. Though opossums usually come out at night, it's not unusual to see one in daylight if they are in search of food or their sleeping quarters are disturbed for some reason.

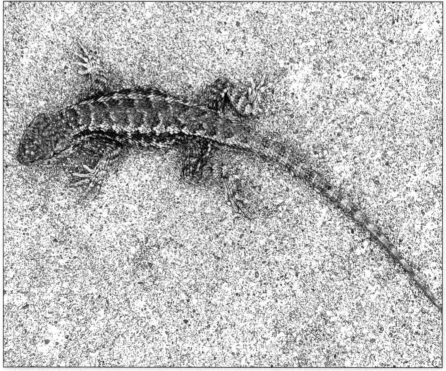

Stagmomantis

"I was within and without, simultaneously enchanted and repelled by the inexhaustible variety of life."

F. Scott Fitzgerald, American novelist and screenwriter

July 24

Stagmomantis are in abundance here and I often see them in the courtyard. Their common name, Praying Mantis, includes the Greek word for prophet or fortune teller, due to their upright posture. You can see their long claws, tapered body, and huge eyes, and they can also camouflage themselves. What you usually don't see is their diet, which includes other insects such as bees, butterflies, smaller flying bugs, and those previously mentioned lizards, of which we have many. They also prey on small birds, including hummingbirds and sparrows. They can also fly, and have you seen a really close up photo? I'm glad they are small.

The most striking behavior of all, at least for the female Praying Mantis, is that she will typically eat the male after mating. Yikes!

Toms, Hens, and Poults

"Turkeys, quails, and small birds, are here to be seen..."

William Bartram, American botanist, ornithologist, natural historian, and explorer

The turkeys have been seen everywhere—perhaps filling the void more than ever since the geese are now gone. We've seen late-season baby turkeys (poults), and daily, we count the remaining ones as the hawks pick them off.

As for the toms, they come around in groups in front of our business windows during mating season and do the turkey trot with their puffed up bodies and tail feathers spread out. The hens are often seen resting on a hot day under the trees or eating in the grass or nearby hill.

Arturo told me of a poult he had rescued. It seems the little creature had fallen into a ground depression while her family moved on. So as not to put the human smell on the poult, Arturo put on heavy work gloves and managed to get the little bird out of trouble. He searched and found the family, and after encouraging her to reunite with her mom and siblings, witnessed a happy welcoming.

Oh, and the turkeys eat any small moving thing on the ground, including the Stagmomantis.

Photo by Arturo Sandoval

The Hawk and the Sparrow

"Look at the sparrows; they do not know what they will do in the next moment. Let us literally live from moment to moment."

Mahatma Gandhi, Indian lawyer and political ethicist

August 14

Later in August, long after the geese had gone, I saw a Cooper's hawk perched in a tree. She is strikingly beautiful and dangerous, like the resident apex, top of the food chain predator that she is.

I know hawks can perch for hours, sometimes taking off to hunt and then returning to perch once again in the same spot. I had seen her as I walked through the corridor and felt sure she was the same hawk we encountered last year. She was enjoying the afternoon right outside the window until a little sparrow landed on the branch next to her. I was horror-stricken until I realized that even with their talons out, a hawk needs some glide path to fall on its prey at high speeds from the sky.

There was no chance of a fast glide from one branch to reach the sparrow on the next, and I think the little bird somehow knew that. Could that be why that bird seemed to taunt the hawk all the more by its mere presence?

I watched for quite a while until the hawk had had just about enough and opened her slightly curved beak and screeched her discontent. The sound was so piercing that it reverberated inside where I was standing. Even after that impressive display, the little sparrow just sat there. If I were that bird, I'd fear the hawk's powerful presence. The bird could have easily flown to another branch out of sight of the hawk. Instead, it was the hawk who ended this tête-à-tête and leapt with a single bound across the courtyard, lost from sight in some trees on the other side, probably settling in for another long perching session.

It's interesting to note that the hawk abandoned her nest this year. We presume she did so because her eyas fell out of her own nest in an oppressive heat wave last year. Her babies were rescued while the hawk was away making her rounds, so she could not have known what happened. Perhaps she felt that nest area was no longer safe. Still, she did not go far and frequently made her presence known to every living creature in her territory. One courageous, if not sneaky little squirrel, investigated the empty nest. Maybe he was well aware there was no recent hawk activity and guessed that it was safe.

The Geese Press On—
Where there's Smoke there's Fire

"Calligraphy of geese against the sky—the moon seals it."

Yosa Buson, Japanese poet and painter of the Edo period

August 21

California has a yearly fire season, and this year it wreaked havoc beyond imagination. People lost their lives, their homes, and their animals. Everyone knew someone who was affected in some way. Working at a data center, we heard of several business tragedies, as well as the success stories from those who had been proactive in their disaster recovery planning. We also witnessed much bravery and people coming together.

One of the secondary problems of fires is the effect on air quality. Though the fires raged hundreds of miles away, the smoke filled our skies and darkened them for weeks. We prayed for rain, but the rainy season was far off.

One day I was heading home for the evening into a smoky landscape that looked not unlike like Mars, and there in the distance, across the sky, I saw a skein, the v-formation of Canada geese. Every time I see such a sight, I feel like good luck is washing over me. Indeed, I feel lucky to live and work along their flyway. I do, however, wonder how they fared, breathing in the smoke as we did on the ground. Even in this bittersweet confluence of time, it was the perfect moment to be alive, to drink it in, and to be touched with the indescribable magnificence of the Canada goose.

Photo by Gordon Serviss

Year Three: A Sneak Peek

"Once again we waited. It had been just over six months since we'd last seen them. The lifespan of Canada geese is 10-24 years, and we had already learned from the past two years that they are philopatric, derived from the Greek "home loving" or returning to the same site. That meant that the mated pair of Canada geese could visit our enclosed courtyard for many more years to come.

Expectations began to run high as we noticed an occasional pair of geese frequently flying above, or a wedge of geese, or geese in V-formation.

We were two weeks into the third year. A cold rain was pouring down non-stop when our friends finally appeared and it was nothing short of magical."

"There were still no hatched goslings, but workers had appeared early in the morning before I arrived and placed a fence around Mother Goose. There was room around her, but this was not a good development. The fence was made of soft black plastic with white metal posts stuck deep in the ground. On a narrow strip of concrete behind her that ran the length of the courtyard as well as the length of the glassed-in corridor from where we watched, two strips of steel were bolted to the ground. That's where the fence was immovably affixed.

Mother Goose was unhappy and she hissed the entire time of construction. The workers were just following orders.

These are good people and their actions were based on good intentions. Yet, all the people who saw Mother Goose fenced in, knew this was more than an injustice, even though they knew she could readily fly out. I couldn't stand back and accept this situation. First, Canada geese are federally protected: It is illegal to harm geese, their eggs, or their nests in the United States. The Migratory Bird Treaty Act protects both resident and migratory Canada geese in all four international treaties. This would include our geese. That is reason enough to remove the fencing.

By Tuesday morning, one of the goslings had slipped underneath the fence, and all hell broke loose as the parents honked wildly not able to help."

Resources

Informative Facts and websites about the Canada goose

"The greatness of a nation and its moral progress can be judged by the way its animals are treated."

Mahatma Gandhi, Indian lawyer and political ethicist

- People often call the bird a Canadian goose, but its proper name is Canada goose and its Latin name is Branta Canadensis.
- Canada geese can fly at night.
- Canada geese have great memories, using landmarks to reach their destination.
- Canada geese have 12 times more photoreceptive cones in their retina at the back of the eye than humans.
- Canada geese see color.
- While still in the egg, goslings can communicate with their parents with greeting "peeps."
- Geese also communicate with "body language."
- The female chooses her mate by following a male around or standing next to him continually.
- She chooses her mate based on his demonstrated ability to protect her.
- When chosen, the male will start to defend the area around his new mate.

Audubon Society
https://www.audubon.org/field-guide/bird/canada-goose

Wildlife – California Rice
https://calrice.org/california-geese-101/

National Geographic
https://kids.nationalgeographic.com/animals/birds/facts/canada-goose

Washington Department of Fish and Wildlife
https://wdfw.wa.gov/species-habitats/species/branta-canadensis

Humane Society of the United States
https://www.humanesociety.org/animals/geese

Library of Congress
https://www.loc.gov/everyday-mysteries/item/why-do-geese-fly-in-a-v/

Citizens for the Preservation of Wildlife
http://www.preservewildlife.com/canada-geese.html

Salthaven Canada Goose Roof Top Rescue
https://www.youtube.com/watch?v=oon0k5qvLkU

Fly Away Home
https://www.imdb.com/video/vi3265724697

Wildlife Care Association
http://www.wildlifecareassociation.com/

UC Davis Veterinary Medicine
https://ohi.vetmed.ucdavis.edu/centers/california-raptor-center

Beauty of Birds
https://www.beautyofbirds.com/canadageese.html
A great site for a strong overall summary of Canada geese including:
- "Canada geese are native to:
  Americas: Canada, Greenland, United States, Mexico. * Islands: Bahamas, Cayman Islands, Cuba, Haiti, Puerto Rico, Saint Pierre and Miquelon, Turks and Caicos Islands * Asia: Kamchatka Peninsula in eastern Siberia, eastern China, and throughout Japan."

- "Canada geese have been introduced to:
  Austria, Belgium, Czech Republic, Faroe Islands, Finland, France, Germany, Ireland, Netherlands, New Zealand, Poland, Russian Federation, Ukraine, Great Britain and Scandinavia (Denmark, Norway and Sweden)

  Great Britain: (These geese were introduced into England about 300 years ago, where it is now the most recognized goose species. It is less common in Scotland and Wales)."

- "Canada geese can either be truly migratory or resident (non-migratory).
  Those occurring in temperate/mild climates may choose to remain year-around in their home range, due to adequate winter food supply and a lack of predators. However, even those populations that don't migrate south for the winter, will move north after the breeding season to a safe area for the yearly molt, which lasts about a month.

  Some migratory populations no longer travel as far south in the winter as they used to. These changes in migration are attributed to changes in weather patterns, changes in farm practices that make waste grain readily available in fall and winter, as well as changing hunting pressure.

  Over the last decade, the numbers of migratory Canada geese have seen a decline, whereas resident populations have seen near exponential growth."

- In Swedish, Canada geese are called, Kanadagås.
  "The hatching chicks break out of the shell by using an "egg tooth" - a hard growth on top of their beaks, which diminishes not long after hatching. It may take 8-36 hours for them to completely break out of the shell (French and Parkhurst, 2001)."

  "Their bill has lamellae (miniature ridges inside the bills of water feeding birds or "teeth") around the outside edges of the bill that are used as a cutting tool."

- "Canada Geese have an extensive range in northern temperate, sub-arctic and arctic regions. They are found throughout Canada, Alaska and all the lower 48 U.S. states, as well as northern Mexico… The migratory populations travel south to Florida, the Gulf Coast, and northern Mexico for the winter. Many populations occurring in the temperate regions are resident (non-migratory)."

Canada geese make many sounds, including honking, cooing, chattering, chirping and chiming, they also tweet.
https://video.search.yahoo.com/search/video?fr=mcafee&ei=UTF-8&p=sounds+of+canada+geese+youtube&type=E211US739G0#id=3&vid=4eaa6b39a7665bdae2da19a381f88a61&action=click

Thousands of Canadian Geese (and Mallard Ducks) - Flying Away and Sounds
https://www.youtube.com/watch?v=TldwEY5ukPc

Rescuing gosling
https://www.youtube.com/watch?v=2fU4WF40W74

National Geographic Video
https://www.youtube.com/watch?v=5QAjfH05IUE
Breathtaking video of the "birdman," Christian Moullec, a former meteorologist, who cares for orphaned geese (and other avians) from birth, then takes people on a microlight plane to fly with them.

Earthflight - BBC One
https://www.youtube.com/watch?v=mrO4dvUest4

Along Came Ryan, the Little Gosling King
https://www.youtube.com/watch?v=XqK23IMkIr0
Watch Mother Goose, Hawkeye and their four goslings eating in the enclosed courtyard.

Love Canada Geese
http://www.lovecanadageese.com/
The website authors are located in Canada with a huge international following of goose lovers. You will find beautiful photos, stories, and much more.
- "Every goose also has his/her individual personality, just like your pets, family or friends…Some are loud; others are quiet. Some rush about like running backs or battle tanks; others move gracefully, with head held high…"

- "They're a lot of fun to watch when they take nesting breaks. They cover their eggs with down and grass, then race to their mates, who are overwhelmed with happiness to be with them again. Together, they honk as they fly into the water where she dips and bathes herself, drinks, feeds, stretches, chases other geese for exercise, and is as happy and active as she can be. Nesting breaks are short, usually lasting about ten minutes though some geese take long breaks of an hour or more, and soon, she trots back to her nest, stands dripping over her eggs while she preens herself, plucks soft down from her breast to line her nest, and then settles down to continue incubating her eggs."

Maidu Museum, Roseville, CA offering walking tours with displays of Maidu artifacts, original indigenous art, and basketry.
https://eventseeker.com/venue/821433-maidu-museum-historic-site-roseville

Roseville Historical Society offers a wealth of information about Roseville. The organization oversees the Carnegie Library Museum housed in a 106-year-old building, now on the National Register of Historic Places.
http://www.rosevillehistorical.org/

Courtyard between Quest and Cokeva

"Alone we can do so little, together we can do so much"

Helen Keller, American author and lecturer

Hawkeye and Mother Goose

About the Author

Barbara Klide was born in New York City and graduated with an MBA from Golden Gate University, San Francisco, and a Certificate in Graphic Design from the University of California, Davis. She is the Director of Marketing for Quest Technology Management, California.

It was at this firm where she was presented the opportunity for discovery of the mated pair of elegant, sensitive, and smart Canada geese and their goslings who nested several years in a row in the corporate courtyard. Her skills in observation and compassion coupled with writing and design allowed her to bring this amazing story to others who also find interest and excitement about wildlife in our midst.

Her early writings about this remarkable pair and their offspring drew much interest from several including Dr. Lorin Lindner, PhD, Wolves and Warriors, (*Animal Planet*) and Bill Bianco, President, Audubon Society, Sacramento. Barbara donates a portion of the book profits to various wildlife rescue groups.

Barbara is also a contributing author to several anthologies published by the Northern California Publishers and Authors Association (NCPA) including *Destination: The World*, Volumes One and Two; *All Holidays*, 2020 and 2021, and *More Birds of a Feather*, 2019.

Barbara is a dedicated ballroom dancer at the Silver level through Arthur Murray International, Inc. She and her longtime partner reside in Northern California where they rescue, foster, and adopt out cats. They are the recipients of the oft awarded "foster failure" badge for giving in to kitty demands to remain in the foster residence, staking claim as their very own forever home—a most satisfactory arrangement for all.

For more photos, videos and information, visit www.BarbaraKlide.com